Prisoner of Purpose
Ditch the Escape Plan and Live a Powerful Life

Rob Boyd

Copyright © 2025 by Rob Boyd

All rights reserved. No part of this book may be reproduced or used in any manner without written permission of the copyright owner except for the use of quotations in a book review. For more information, address: info@therobboyd.com

First Edition; May 2025

Book cover design by Rica Graphics

ISBN 979-8-9921652-1-0

www.therobboyd.com

Published by: Boyd Solutions LLC

Dedication

To my grandmother, Jean Boyd. For my brothers that fell on the road to living out our dreams, Chris Turner and Jalil Stokes. Your lives pushed me to be purposeful.

Visit **www.therobboyd.com** online!

LEARN MORE about Rob
Tap in and stay informed! Check out his personal website that provides recent news, blog posts, and booking information. You can also find the various ways to connect with Rob on social media!

Table of Contents

Acknowledgements............................6
Preface..8
Introduction..................................15

1. Finding Yourself..............................19
2. The Wake Up Call............................27
3. The Battle vs the War.......................36
4. Ditching the Escape Plan....................46
5. God in You......................................55
6. Using Your Time..............................61
7. Trusting Alignment..........................67
8. Protect The Mission.........................77

About the Author............................84

Acknowledgements

Thank you to all that inspired, motivated, listened, and supported me.

I would like to show my deepest gratitude to my Mom for her unwavering support, encouragement, and belief in me throughout this journey. Your endless patience, understanding, and love have been my pillars of strength.

A special thank you to my family! Dad, Austin Anderson, Zari Ivey, Josh Worthy, Angela Anderson, Levon Boyd, Wanda Worthy, Deneen Ivey, Audrey Boyd, LaVerne Stevens, Tatyana White, Markquel Stevens, Alana Boyd, Jenaya Howard, Anika Anderson, Dekenia Norfleet, Kent Stevens, Tiera Cox, Eunice Stevens, Jeff McCullough, Momma Fox, James Worthy, Miyanda Anderson, and last but not least my little brother Tae Norfleet. Thank you all for the never ending support and for making every family event a memorable moment.

I am also grateful to the countless individuals who contributed to my life as a friend, business partner, motivator, classmate, or teammate. Ashley Fox, Lawrence "LB" Charles, Phil Clancy, Jasmine Hopkins, Dr. Charles Bell, Loyan Mensah, Hasan Asad, Andrew Jones, Maxx Pamphile, Jennifer Robinson, Houston Jackson, Chris Munn, Reni Jackson, Brendon Henderson, Dr. Ella Washington, Jamal Washington, Corey Evans, Kishanda Oliver, Ash Cash Exantus, Nehemiah Davis, Marshall Williams, Dominique Sutton, Preston Smith, Marcus Ingram, Greg Hill, Bobby

Hudgins, Yannick Braimbridge, Joya Williams, Jamesha Clanton, Kymshya Jones, Joey Womack, Paul Adamson, C'Vonzell Dondrico, Jamal "Tip" Stewart, Utahya Drye, Jeron Smith, Shelly Andrews, Reesey Robinson, Trent Bivens, Ron Branch, Tyree Graham, Weslye Saunders, Jordan "Pardi" Thorpe, Brandon Ruffin, Pher Harris, Leslie White, Mark Williams, Aminata Sow, Jasmyn Burke, Mahailla Ricketts, Brock Young, Siedah Garrett-Guess, Katona Payne, BJ White, Leander Pickett, Ashley Maltbia, Maria Barlow, Shauntey Hall, Tanya Turrentine, Lyndon Gray, Olivia Clancy, Dan Gilfort, John Wall, and John Thomas.

To my coaches and mentors, thank you for your guidance at times when I didn't know I needed it! Coach Reed, Gary Rappaport, Coach Vic, Coach Teets, Dr. Gregory Carr, Prof. William Spriggs, Bob Proctor, Tony Robbins, and Ed Mylett. You all pushed me in ways that I hated sometimes but I am forever grateful.

It is my sincere hope that this book brings you joy, enlightenment, or whatever you seek within its pages.

Again, I dedicate this book to my Grandma who saved the day so many times throughout my life. Your impact on my life is immeasurable, and this book is a tribute to your love and guidance.

Thank you all, from the depths of my heart, for being a part of this journey.

Preface

I grew up spending most of my childhood years in a single-parent household in Durham, NC. When I was elementary I learned that I was different from the kids. My mind worked differently. There were moments that I suppressed my genius to fit in but also moments like the National Geography Bee where I destroyed the competition easily. My mom had a unique battle as a parent. She had to balance allowing me to find my way with protecting me from the realities of the streets. My hometown city is plagued with gang violence and crime most of which is a product of decreasing economic opportunities.

At the age 8, I found myself building lego sets in minutes, watching National Geographic, and mastering Number Munchers. While I knew something was different about me, I also saw my mom crying over past due bills. She saw my intelligence early on too. The guilt she carried for not being able to afford a computer was something I noticed before I really knew the definition of guilt. I simply saw her body language as I described a math game that I played at school that I had no ability to play at home. Deep down she wanted to feed my genius in any way possible. She knew it was our ticket out of financial strife.

Things started to change in middle school. Not so much the financial piece but the environment around me. My everyday surroundings started to take shape but positively and negatively. I remember several teachers pushing me to go further scholastically and push my mind. Alternatively, I had teachers that couldn't understand why I didn't "show my work" on math problems or why I slept through classes yet aced the tests. The lack of challenge simply bored me. Every other week I was in ISS with the forgotten kids. Those that had life challenges that the school system didn't acknowledge. In those ISS class trailers, I found friends. Kids that felt misunderstood like I did. Kids that started turning to gangs for acceptance and camaraderie.

There I was, "mentally gifted" but behaviorally insubordinate. It was in this phase of life I started to embody the idea of leading the outsiders. Being the one that understood the rules but knew enough to beat them without playing by them. I began to view the world's structures as the problem more than how my brain was designed.

I fully understood that it was better to be smart than dumb, however I didn't want to be known as the smart kid. There was no protection in being the focal point. The hood conditioned me to think that the ones that stand out often end up on a shirt, whether their endeavors were positive or negative. The good die young while the infamous have a short reign at the top. I was conditioned to believe the "middle" survived. Therefore, I played the middle but with a big heart and sharp mind.

Simply put, I didn't like the attention of being the smartest in the room. To the point that I found a lane in which I could start from the "middle," basketball. My *purpose* knocked on the door again in high school when I found myself as one of the best players on the team and unanimously chosen as the team captain. Leading was easy. I was always several steps ahead mentally. I thought about things that didn't naturally cross the minds of others. Considered outcomes that no one could see at any given moment in time. That garnered trust and belief from my peers. "Rob knows, ask him."

While I found my way in basketball, I couldn't help but notice childhood friends and neighborhood stars falling from grace. There was an unfortunate set of realities setting in for people I was in the sandbox with. High school dropouts, juvenile delinquency, and even untimely deaths were more prevalent than ever. Outside of Poe Gymnasium, life was happening and it was real. After a session in the North (Durham), I remember pulling up to Bojangles with the homies with life on my mind. I turned to my bro Chris (CT) and told him "we gotta get out of Durham before it kills us". No clue why that came to mind in the moment but CT turned to me and said "you ain't f*ckin lying bro". That line still rings in my head daily after losing him to the streets of Durham years later.

Today, Durham is a place of lost dreams. Historically, it's known by many as "Black Wall Street" or the home of the Hayti community which both illustrated the power of unity in the early 1900s. Now it's a shell of that. Gang rivalries, rap beefs, and the *crab in a bucket* mentality keeps progress from being common. Too often, young gifted children fall to the wayside and become memories to those that knew they had so much more life to live. This reality ultimately led me to leave Durham to get a break from the stressful events in my hometown. College seemed to be my one and only exit strategy. An injury before my senior year of high school slowed my basketball momentum but luckily my mind was still sharp.

One of the great experiences that made me who I am today is Howard University. It's actually the only school I applied to.

In college, I found my genius. At Howard, everyone was gifted in some form or fashion, EVERYONE. Some of the smartest Black teenagers in the world were on Howard's campus. I knew I was one of them but wasn't quite sure how this chapter of life would play out. One thing I was sure of is that Durham built me to prevail in any situation.

Still, there was still an unshakeable question.

Who am I? It's a question I've wrestled with my entire life, 36 years on this earth. I've finally learned who I am because I'm not Rob Boyd, that's just my name.

Who I am to the core is something way deeper than just a name. I've lived through losses. I've lived to win. At this stage, I'm just here to live. To experience things in a way that my spirit needs to experience them. I know that sounds deep. Let me give you a backdrop.

As I stated before I grew up in the city with most people that look like me are dead or in jail by age 25. Throughout my life, I've learned that it's not the moment that decides who you are. It's how you respond to the moments.

I've lost people. I've seen negative balances in my bank account. I've been beat out for opportunities. I've walked away from thriving businesses. I've started over. It's those moments that hurt the most that actually prepare you to thrive. There was a knowing I possessed that reassured me that I would endure. I've learned that others have this feeling too. It's like a voice in your head that says "I'm gonna ultimately win". Prisoner of Purpose will articulate the feelings and nuances in a way that will reassure you!

Success leaves clues and you are justified in wanting to get a blueprint to life from someone that's living in their wins. Prayerfully, my list of accomplishments is not slim:

- Top 500 Financial Leaders in the US (2014)
- One of the youngest to open financial advisory office in DC
- Served over 300 financial advisory clients to create over $60M in generational wealth
- Consulted and guided 70+ regional and large banks
- International speaker with over 15 speaking engagements with universities, Fortune 500 companies, and economic development agencies, and more
- Tony Robbins Inner Circle trainee
- Created financial programs and content that has helped over 500,000 people
- Licensed USA Basketball® youth coach
- Educated beginner investors to actively invest over $11.5M in 3 years

- and more....

I've often been called a quiet one, the reserved one the one that doesn't talk much, which may be true. But, I was always watching. I was observing the game. When I say "the game", the game of life. I study how other people have won. I've studied why certain individuals have lost. Not to judge them, but to make sure I stepped up in a way that I would never resent or regret how I approached life as an adult and as a professional.

I've also seen a variety of things that I never imagined experiencing as a child. I've been in boardrooms outlining business strategies plans with bank executives. I've shown multimillion dollar real estate developers the real estate opportunities in top markets. However, I've also sat across the table from everyday families with hundreds of people and mapped out their financial life. Just to make it clear, we're not here to talk about finance.

I'm here to share a story, an epiphany that will equip you for life. I think it will resonate with every single person in this world. A story about *purpose*, a story about understanding why to fight and how to endure the journey of life.

I learned from my defining moments and I know you've had your fair share too. I have been at *rock bottom* and I learned that it is the firmest place to stand. Now that I've gotten everything back that I ever lost plus more, I realize it's not what I know or what

I've learned scholastically that helped me get it all back.

You may not know exactly why you're reading this book yet but as you read it, I promise there will be a lightbulb moment. You'll realize something that you probably didn't think you were going to realize.

It took me 36 years to write this book. Every single day, week, month, and year mattered. I'm playing with house money. I've won. I beat the odds already. This is about sharing codes to win!

I'm living solely on purpose at this point. I know the value that I bring to the world will always create the value that I need to live in it.

Introduction

Life will beat your ass if you let it. You can feel like you were born into a situation that has stacked the odds against you. When facing challenges that you did not create or invite into your life, you will often look for a guiding light. Hence, you may engage in practices to uplift yourself spiritually, mentally, and emotionally.

In the midst of these practices, you will find your own ways to contribute. You may stumble upon these or actively search for ways to empower or give to others. To keep it simple, we'll call them acts of purpose.

Purposeful living is seemingly the simplest path to fulfillment. To your core, you want to be valuable to the people you love or serve.

> *Instead of counting the days, make the days count.*

Muhammed Ali was spot on in that quote and it embodies what your innate goal is.

The challenge lives in the notion that as an individual with a unique background, intelligence, and set of experiences you may not be clear on your unique contribution to the world. This contribution is often labeled as your purpose.

I found how I would make my *contribution* as a result of events and circumstances that I wouldn't wish on anyone else. In fact, this book took me 9 years to write. Did it have to take that long? Of course not. But I also needed time to become the person that could confidently deliver a message that will change the trajectory of my life forever.

The timeline of events that has provided me with the experiences to share the message in this book started in January 2000. When I was a 11, I had a great uncle pass away and my family gathered at his house before the service. A family friend that was also a pastor stopped by. Personally, I had never met her before and to this day do not remember her name. A few minutes after she spoke to all of the adults, she came up to me and said "I don't know what it is but you're going to do something special in life" and simply walked away. That moment stuck with me my entire life and I randomly think about that moment and wonder where that lady is. I was unaware at that point in time but looking back, her words created a sense of self awareness that has contributed to this book being possible.

I grew up in a city known for positive and negative highlights, Durham, North Carolina. Dating back to the early 1900s, Durham was a thriving metropolis for Black business owners known as "Black Wall Street"

However, a hundred years later, it has been plagued by gangs and gun violence that has placed it in the ranks of most dangerous cities in America. Oddly enough, much of this activity was normal to me growing up. I thought most cities had the problems that Durham had.

I started to see my environment differently as the words from that lady constantly replayed in my mind

...You're going to do something special in life

This was the earliest instance of me unknowingly learning about the power of purpose. My great uncle passed away when I was in middle school. At the time, I was going to a school outside of the district so I rode the city bus everyday to get home. This introduced me to what many would call the ugly side of Durham. I got acquainted with some of the city's most infamous gangs around the age of 12. I didn't feel out of place nor did I feel like a target. It was just the reality of the environment around me.

I remember sitting on the city bus everyday after school thinking about those words. Leaving Githens Middle School, I hopped on the #17 to the downtown bus terminal then got on the #9 to go to North Durham. It might sound like a normal two bus journey on paper but these two routes went through neighborhoods of rivaling gangs. I saw it all. Fights, shootings, drug addicts, robberies. It was commonplace on various afternoons in Durham and I got used to it.

On many of those rides, I was curious about what this *special* thing in life was going to be. What's most interesting is that instead of being persuaded or recruited into a gang like many others were, I laughed and joked with the people that I was encouraged to avoid. At the end of the day, we were all young black kids just finding our way.

I didn't know it then but now I realize there was purpose in those connections. I would ultimately become an example of what was possible in a positive way although I came from negative environments. Playing sports in high school vaulted me into a space where I was protected by those very individuals that were deemed as dangerous. It all made sense when I stepped on the campus of Howard University.

I accepted the responsibility to share the message in this book because of the vision that Howard made clear to me. It's not about where you're from, it's not even solely about where you're going. It's about who you are right now and how that is the person that can create every desired outcome of the future.

Chapter 1 - Finding Yourself

We are all on a constant pursuit of purpose. The little known secret is that you do not have to pursue something you already possess. Ask yourself "what if I already have it?" What if the thing I've been looking for was in my pocket the whole time?

You may have been told, or even sold, the idea that you are not in the right place to make the impact that you were meant to make. The amount of time you spend searching for what you were born with is actually startling. Is that time wasted? Not completely. After all, the search itself could be helping you fulfill the purpose that was placed on your heart and soul.

It's not fun realizing that you possess something that you've spent endless hours *searching* for. This perspective could invite an even greater feeling of despair. This is where new thoughts and new people present the solution. Generally, you may have been taught that your environment decides the level of your thoughts. This is true to an extent. However, there's a level of life that could help you accept that your mindset or mentality can overcome any environment. Over time, your thoughts and ideas can completely change your circumstances. Our thinking determines our outcomes on a level that you may not fathom. Deeply suppressed memories can create thoughts that act as barriers in your journey. If there aren't tangible examples of dreams coming into fruition, you might continue to believe that purpose eludes you.

Do you ever think to yourself "how did I get here?" Do you ever seem to be lost in a routine or cycle of undesirable results? This is a space that every person has experienced. When faced with what seems to be insurmountable challenges, there's a tendency to pursue *finding yourself*.

If you ever actually *found* yourself, where do you think you would be hanging out at? It's a common phrase that proves that we forget the power of words. Most times, you'd probably find yourself living a life full of challenges, triumphs, and breakthroughs. That's what life is.

Theoretically, the journey to find yourself is rooted in the idea that you haven't been operating as our best self. Having the awareness that you are not operating at your optimal capacity is an understandable and reasonable realization that's common for many people. However, here's a perspective that may shift your thinking...

As an athlete in organized sports, starting in middle school through college, my identity was wrapped in playing sports. Playing sports is a passion that has provided nurturing environments with coaches, mentors, and positive examples of impactful Black men. Sports protected me from street politics and gave me a reason to care about school. Looking back, I realized that rooting my identity in being a basketball player saved my life.

At times, I even forgot that I was so much more than a basketball player. Especially in high school, basketball gave me privileges that my ego told me I deserved so I looked at the sport as my cheat code to life. Ball was life! Despite having other personal interests, basketball took center stage from ages 11 to 17. Nothing else really mattered. In the summer before my senior year of high school, I had a few opportunities arise to continue basketball on a collegiate level. Ironically, this path to the next level was quickly derailed.

A bad landing in a summer AAU game created a tear in my patellar tendon that brought all of my basketball dreams to a temporary halt. For the first time in my life, I needed to have surgery. I went from "jumping out of the gym" to starting the school year on crutches. This is where I first experienced an identity crisis. I did not know who I would be if basketball was over.

During the recovery process I sat on the couch for days at a time. Thinking about what I would do in life if I wasn't destined to play basketball at a higher level. I was going through the common "find yourself" process. I wasn't truly lost but my body and mind were definitely telling me that. As I navigated a wide range of worst possible thoughts and the best possible outcomes, I remembered that all of my interests weren't related to putting a ball in a hoop with a net.

Here's what I learned from this life-altering event... At some point in history, someone removed a few very important words from the phrase "finding yourself". It should fully read as "**finding the courage to be yourself**"

> *Finding the courage to be yourself in a world full of judgement and opinions is one of most important explorations you could ever commit to*

There's a difficult truth that you must accept. You were never tasked with *finding yourself*. You, personally, were never lost. You simply lost a connection to your inner most desires and got distracted from the vision you have of yourself. Your upbringing is often the source of conditioning that leads you astray. T. Harv Eker, author of Secrets of the Millionaire Mind, explains the form of influences that exist in your life, perfectly. Here are three you should know:

- Verbal programming - What you heard from others
- Modeling - What you saw others do
- Specific incidents - Experiences that shape your emotions or thoughts

These three forms of conditioning have been the foundation to thoughts or behaviors that play a major role in why you feel like you need to "find yourself." People that you love and cherish may have passed you inaccurate information, limiting beliefs, and countless other limitations. It's not because they wanted to hurt you, in many cases, they were trying to protect you from disappointments and mistakes that they themselves have experienced. However, your path is your path. Their guidance could quite possibly land you in a spot where you have to muster up the courage to be yourself. Be the version of you that shifts the plight of generations to come.

There have been, and will be, numerous scenarios that require you to look inward. Accept who you are to yourself and for others.

The underestimation of how your talents, gifts, and passions will make way for you is how you will continue to miss the opportunities to live a fulfilling life.

Sometimes there's a feeling of helplessness or even worse, hopelessness, because you didn't choose your life yet you have to navigate it flawlessly to feel purposeful. Have you ever felt like life threw you on a treadmill on the first day and you somehow missed the training that shows you how to get to your desired destination rather than just run in place?

Good, welcome to the club that we'll call the *human experience*. Everyone feels that the instruction manual for life is missing at some point. You are not alone! However, this notion that your problems are only experienced by you has to be examined. It's as if you think that you're the only person with the challenges you have. Ego is a funny thing. It convinces you that you're special in both convenient and inconvenient ways. It's like a friend that plays both sides. Well, technically that's not a friend. That's a distraction.

Ego is undoubtedly an asset to your life, however it's more useful as the passenger rather than the driver. All of the things you were taught are typically how to use information to make a living. Very rarely will you find people that teach you how to turn the ideas, talents, or God-given gifts into magnets for love, abundance, and prosperity.

The love you show yourself determines the critical things in life. How you love yourself is actually how you will teach others to love you. The experience of happiness is a unique mix of acceptance, positivity, and grace. What does this all mean? You also have to find the courage to <u>love</u> yourself!

One of the blindspots in the "self love" department is the confusing relationship with potential. We often look at our own potential or someone else's potential as a positive thing. *Seeing* potential in yourself, something, or someone else can definitely come from a positive intention or bigger vision, however there's something that is being overlooked. What exactly?... I'm glad you asked.

Potential is what people see when they think what's in front of them isn't good enough.

Yes. Read that again.

Now, think about that. Has a lack of love for the current version of yourself caused you to lean too much on a potential version of you? When you think of the best version of yourself, it can feel like you're far away. The life journey is not about creating a version of you that doesn't already exist. You are you. All you'll ever have is *now*. The focus must be on how to embody your current level of wisdom, knowledge, and understanding. These collective attributes will reshape your life based on you employing those qualities with more consistency. Time does not control your ability to show up for yourself in healthier ways. If there's a belief that a decision to be consistent with "wisdom, knowledge, and understanding" is far away; you may be operating with unhealthy conditioning. You have the liberty to make decisions regardless of circumstances. It's your superpower.

There are three forms of desire that can become the basis of how you view yourself. Simply put, you want to *become, do, or have*. In other words, you want to grow more, take specific actions, or obtain things because there's a belief that you'll love yourself more afterwards.

Newsflash: If you do not love yourself more now, fulfilling the desires in the categories listed above could actually lead to a sense of emptiness. External objects do not create a lasting feeling of purpose. They create a short term excitement from achievement. However, purpose is the flame that warms the soul.

Simply put, self love is a requirement to feeling purpose. You were born with the capacity for gratitude which is closely tied to self love. Life itself is a blessing. The statistical probability of being born proves that you've won the ultimate lottery. In fact, you were chosen to be here.

Your work is simple. Choose to look at your life as a co-creator. You have the evidence required to live like you won the lottery for life. Fulfillment is a product of will, not skill. Use time to choose yourself through gratitude and self love. Appreciate every decision in the past as the basis for the growth and wisdom you've obtained to this point.

Is it a healthy expectation that you'll have this mindset at all times? Probably not. There will be moments when you forget the principles that lead you through hard times. Yet, there's joy in getting back on track; in knowing that you have the power to reset!

Questions to Explore:

- What activities can I do now that my younger self would enjoy?
- Are there things that I do just to avoid being socially awkward?
- What are habits or thoughts that you're beginning to question if they're good for you?
- When you feel/felt "lost", what helped you feel "found"?
- Can you emotionally afford to not love yourself more than anything else in life?

Chapter 2 - The Wake Up Call

When you stay in a hotel and need to be somewhere the next morning, what do you do? Set a wake up call. The convenience is unmatched. It's not many times that you can share the responsibility of waking up at a specific time. However, when the wake up call is unplanned. Life shifts dramatically. It doesn't matter if you're ready. The uncomfortable moments when you are forced to adjust and accept a new reality are actually the first moments of growth.

Pain in an emotional sense typically comes from a loss of love or some type of connection. Ironically, pain can spark growth in ways that help you bring value to the people and things in your life. You have witnessed situations in which breakups, divorces, layoffs, injuries, etc. inspire people to get in shape or pursue a new career path. Pain can be an indicator or sign of what you want to avoid at all costs moving forward. The sheer feeling of pain or discomfort could push you into greatness on its own. One of the most challenging phases of my life showed me the value of pain.

In 2016, so many aspects of my life were being tested. As a young entrepreneur running my own financial advisory office in DC, I faced an issue with a business partner putting me in a compromising situation that forced me to carry the financial responsibility of maintaining an office on my own. The rent, utilities, and more was all on me even though there was an agreement to split the expenses. To the outside world, things looked great. I was winning awards, being honored on stages, and featured in magazine articles yet I was going to sleep every night thinking of a way out. As someone that committed to personal development and leadership trainings early in my career I knew I had to take action to change my situation but I did not know what to do.

For me, that was a problem. I always knew how to guide others in making sound decisions or fixing a problem but I was struggling to do it for myself. After numerous sleepless nights staring at the ceiling, I finally made a decision. I told myself to take a mental break and go to my hometown for a week. My thought was that getting out of the environment of the problem would possibly spark an idea that would take my life into a different direction. Little did I know, the week away from DC would turn into forever.

I recall leaving DC on a Monday afternoon for the 4 hour drive to Durham. During the drive, I don't think I played a second of music. It was one of those silent, thinking drives. I had made this drive so many times during my time attending Howard as a student that I could do the drive on mental autopilot. The entire drive I was thinking of how to live a life that felt more purposeful. The accolades that came along with being one of the *Top 500 Financial Leaders in the US* in 2013 made me feel more empty than I could have ever imagined. That drive was a 4 hour conversation with God asking for a shift. Looking back at it, I was asking for a wake up call that I wasn't ready for.

On the morning of April 14th, 2016, a friend and former teammate Corey called me around 7am with a message that would change everything. My best friend Chris "CT" Turner was killed. The feeling that went through my body was unreal. Even today, I struggle to describe it. Shock, disbelief, anger, and disappointment all at once. Someone I spent everyday with and played in numerous basketball games was suddenly gone.

At this moment, my life was completely turned upside down. The loss made me question myself as a friend, brother, professional, and leader. I cried all day and up until that day I couldn't tell you the last time I cried. Every suppressed frustration, fear, and disappointment came out. Facing the reality that another childhood *brother* was taken was devastating. I was completely lost.

The only thing I had the energy to do was surrender. I told God that I was done fighting. In my mind I had "nothing left". I was depleted physically, mentally, financially, and emotionally.

There were prior moments in my life when I thought my back was against the wall but those paled in comparison to this life changing event. I did not understand what anything in life meant anymore.

The *success* I experienced up until this moment, meaningless. The path forward, unknown. I was stuck.

The gravity of the moment was suffocating. The numerous calls with the same questions... *How are you doing? Do you know who killed Chris? Are you going back to DC?*

I couldn't handle it. I was not ready. I considered changing my number but then I just called Verizon and turned my phone off, completely. I sat in a state of depression for a month. A group of close friends convinced me to get out of NC for my birthday and come up to NYC. I went up on the longest MegaBus ride ever but appreciated the time with them. After those two days, I went right back to Durham and basically locked myself in a room for the entire summer of 2016. During this detachment from the life I knew, I learned so much from stillness.

Everyday I wish CT was still with us but in disguise God gave me exactly what I needed. A reminder. Days are not promised and time spent doing things that are not fulfilling spiritually, mentally, or emotionally will become time lost. The pivotal phase in my life led me to pursue what I truly cared about, which was empowering people with impactful knowledge, not just helping to process financial transactions as an advisor.

The Takeaway

The dark periods in life can birth your brightest revelation. In the time spent replaying past conversations with CT I found a silver lining. I was reminded of every dream, hope, and fear that we talked about. His departure was a wake up call from God, not a hotel's staff member.

Life presents these moments and we often call them "tests". What if it's not a test. Tests are used to determine if you pass or fail. Do you think God needs to test you when he knows what's in your heart? After all, he placed it there. The wake up calls are an opportunity to get up and move with more urgency in the direction that your purpose requires.

It's hard work to take the stance of traumatic events being for your greater good. There's a mental and spiritual maturity you must choose to operate with. This naturally creates space to question yourself or embrace inferiority.

- Why is this happening to me?
- Do I deserve this right now?
- Every time things are going good, something bad happens
- Maybe there isn't more for me than chaos and uncertainty

Here's my contribution to your journey...

Every challenging moment that alters your path in life was placed there to spark your evolution and you have the liberty to choose how you respond to the challenge.

The power of choice is one of the greatest gifts you receive every single day. Don't allow anyone or anything to convince you that you do not have the autonomy to choose *more*, to choose *better*, to choose yourself!

Once you take the stance that in every situation, I get the opportunity to choose what's next. Those moments become a little less paralyzing. Your power is within. I know you've heard that before but it's true.

The *Wake Up Call* is not about if you'll answer, it's about how you'll answer. Will you embrace the idea of being your best self despite the losses or detours you experience? Yes, you have the right to grace. Your immediate response does not have to be rooted in productivity. It can be sadness, anger, or despair. However, after those initial reactions you must choose to be someone that emerges from the rubble as a victor, not a victim. You can claim victory after a loss. That's what makes you great. That a moment does not decide the momentum of your life. In fact, a bad moment can spark an unstoppable momentum towards greater things because of the conversations that you have with yourself in the dark.

List the major wake up calls you've received in life:

Wake Up Call	What were the initial emotions you felt?	How do you view the wake up call now?

Four Steps to Reclaiming Your Journey After a Wake Up Call

The trauma in the events you mentioned above could trap you in doubt and fear. However, you are resilient to the core. No matter how long you may pause on the journey of life, you are not restricted from forward progress. Here are four transformative steps that can rekindle the light of purpose and direction: Growth, Choice, Acceptance, and Embrace.

Growth: Leaning Into Inner Resilience
In the aftermath of trauma, it is natural to feel uprooted. Yet, every experience, no matter how challenging, holds the potential for growth. This growth doesn't imply forgetting the past; rather, it involves integrating the experience into our personal narrative and allowing it to enhance your resilience. Start by acknowledging the pain and recognizing the

lessons it holds. Just like a tree after the winter, you too can emerge stronger, with deeper roots and a broader perspective. This conscious effort to expand your emotional depth can be the first step toward healing.

Choose: Reclaiming Your Power

Traumatic events can often leave you feeling powerless, as if the control of your life has slipped through our fingers. However, every moment presents a choice—a chance to steer your own course. Choose to take small, deliberate steps toward restoring your power to choose. Whether it's embracing a new routine, making healthier lifestyle choices, or pursuing long-neglected passions, these decisions signify your determination to move forward. Remember, choosing is an act of empowerment. By consciously shaping your path, you reclaim control over your future.

Accept: Finding Peace with Your Story

Acceptance is not synonymous with resignation. It is simply an acknowledgment of what has occurred and a commitment to move beyond it. This entails recognizing the parts of your life that cannot be changed and making peace with them. Acceptance frees you from the burden of resistance and allows you to channel your energy toward what is possible. By accepting your story, you honor your journey and allow yourself to heal. This newfound sense of peace can be the foundation for building a future that isn't limited by the scars of the past.

Embrace: Welcoming New Possibilities

As you navigate the path to recovery, embracing change becomes a pivotal step and ultimately a skill. Embrace the new, unexplored possibilities that lie ahead, and cultivate a mindset open to the newness of things you may attract as you move forward. Consider this an opportunity to redefine yourself and your aspirations. Approach each day with curiosity and courage, welcoming the growth that comes from stepping into the unknown. Embrace not only change, but also the person you are becoming—more resilient, more compassionate, and more aware of the boundless potential within you.

In the journey of rediscovery or in finding the courage to be yourself again, remember that the power to reshape your destiny is within you. As you walk this path with intention and courage, you unlock the door to a renewed sense of purpose. By committing to these four steps—Growth, Choice, Acceptance, and Embrace—you create a roadmap for healing and transformation, guiding you back on track to a life full of amazing experiences and illuminated by a newfound understanding of yourself.

Chapter 3 - The Battle vs the War

Understanding the Opponent

Honestly, we are miseducated from the beginning of our lives as to why we're here, who we are, and what matters. You could even travel the depths of the rabbit holes on YouTube to find the ways in which you're distracted from living purposefully.

Your value as an adolescent is often based on how you compare to others. Think about elementary school, our names are called in alphabetical order to determine our presence. As a pre-teen or teenager, your grades or performance in sports determines your value. Even amongst siblings there's a battle for superiority. What do all of these examples have in common? They require a comparison to other people!

In this conditioning, especially during our formative years, we fall into the battle of being better than others.

In our formative years, between the ages of 8 to 14, we are on a journey of self-discovery and development. This is a crucial time in our lives where we begin to create our own identity and develop a perspective of how we want to live our lives.

During this time, you may start to become more aware of your surroundings and begin to question the world around you. Our age and maturity begin to play a significant role in shaping our thoughts and actions. As we enter puberty and start to navigate through the complexities of becoming a teenager, we are bombarded with new experiences, emotions, and challenges that test our self-esteem and intelligence.

The opinions and values of our peers and family members may influence you, but ultimately, it is your own beliefs and choices that shape your identity. Whether you knew it or not, you started to develop a sense of self-worth and self-esteem, which forms the basis of your confidence and decision-making abilities.

Your intelligence, whether street smarts or book smarts, also plays a vital role in this stage of life. In many scenarios you begin to ponder concepts and ideas, and your curiosity may drive you to explore new things. This is the age where we start to understand the consequences of your actions and how they can impact your life and those around you.

You can get stuck on the battleground known as comparison. Don't get me wrong, there's a thrill in competing for attention or acknowledgement. However, the thrill is shallow and temporary. Soon, you'll be on the quest for the next short lived battle or win. The law of diminishing returns creeps in. Allow me to explain this theory because it will explain so many occurrences in life.

Quick explanation:

One of the greatest turning points in my life was learning that I had a knack for economics in Dr. Spriggs Macroeconomics class at Howard University. The *Law of Diminishing Returns* jumped off the page and I understood it immediately. At its core, this law illustrates a fundamental truth about human nature and experience: the once thrilling tastes, sounds, and sights inevitably begin to fade. They are subject to a dwindling sparkle in our eyes, no matter how captivating they might have been initially.

Imagine biting into a ripe, juicy apple. The first taste is a symphony of crispness and sweetness, an unparalleled delight. But as you continue to consume, each subsequent bite yields slightly less pleasure than the one before, until the apple's brilliance becomes a mere background thought... a routine taste.

This is the essence of diminishing returns, a concept that transcends economic theory and infiltrates the very fabric of your life. You remember the first time driving your new car? The interior smell, the clean exterior, the full tank. It was an amazing feeling at first but after a few months and even a detailed wash, that initial feeling never comes back.

The process of gratification dwindling over time is not exclusive to consumption. Consider the rush of a new romantic relationship or friendship. The initial months can feel like an exhilarating ascent, driven by connection, discovery, and possibly infatuation. It's often called the honeymoon phase. However, as days turn into weeks and weeks into months, the thrilling heights temper into comforting familiarity. The excitement that once electrified every moment begins to settle into routine patterns. This doesn't diminish the relationship's value but reshapes it; the law teaches us that new novelties are vital to sustaining lasting engagement.

In creativity, this principle provides a profound lesson. The first spark of genius may ignite your artistic endeavors, but as we repeatedly tread the same inspirational ground, the initial fervor wanes. Recognizing this natural decline can empower you to seek fresh perspectives or experiences. Or to continuously reinvent and rejuvenate your approach to the mundane aspects of your life.

The law of diminishing returns invites us to think about ourselves in deeper ways. How can we harness understanding of this principle to find enduring satisfaction? It's an opportunity to become architects of our happiness, sculpting a reality of varied experiences rather than relying on singular passions.

In conclusion, while the law of diminishing returns may at first appear as a cautionary tale of decline, it is, in truth, a catalyst for evolution. This so-called evolution will cause you to not be as fixated on the smaller battles but to actually acknowledge the actual war. It challenges you to pivot, innovate, and reinvent. *Now back to the story...*

The *Wake Up Call* is the moment in which you become aware that your calling is to show up for the *war* instead of simply finding thrill in the battle. At this point you have to ask yourself, WHAT IS THE WAR?

The war is the lifelong process of fighting the temptation to compete with the people and things in your life.

You can't compete where you don't compare.

The "war" is a *you vs you* thing. You have to decide that you're better than you were yesterday. You in fact have one more day of experience than you had yesterday. It's in your nature to take the opportunity to lead your life. It's the "battle" type of distractions that derail you.

Sounds good, but what does that really mean?! It means trusting your intuition, your heart, your gift. Instead of focusing on what others will think, you begin to focus on how you'll feel. Even with that said, you may look for a compromise. Your thoughts will tell you, "if others like what I'm doing or what I have, I'll feel accomplished and satisfied". That's battlefield thinking. It's time to move like a General, not a soldier.

Imagine a life where your leading thought is "will pursuing this goal help me have a greater sense of love for myself?" That's General talk!

Here's where your conditioning gets in the way. When choosing that line of thinking for the first time. Ideas of lack infiltrate your mind. Here's are examples of things that come to mind when your newly practiced focus on your internal experience is in motion:

- *I have bills. Is this going to help me survive right now?*
- *The last time I put myself first, I lost relationships that I valued*
- *This is crazy. Nothing I ever do works. I need to come back to reality before I set myself back*

Those examples are just the tip of the iceberg. This list is never ending. Keep in mind, many of these thoughts are not yours. You've picked them up from people along the way. Let's call them borrowed thoughts that you decided to own. That's no fault of your own until you have the awareness that how others view obstacles does not create the standard for how you view them. Again, remember the impact of conditioning.

Winning the War

There are steps to winning the war. Stephen Covey highlights a powerful statement in The 7 Habits of Highly Effective People.

"It is said that wars are won in the general's tent"

This proverbial tent is your mind. Your job is to organize your thoughts in a way that allows you to act confidently in alignment with your soul. The steps are simple.

Step 1	Acknowledge your *battlefield* thinking
Step 2	Assess the gratification you get from battles
Step 3	Determine your goals in *war*
Step 4	Trust yourself to commit to the internal victories

Step 1

This can be the hardest step. Coming to grips with how you've been driven by external forces is not fun. You may realize that you've spent years meeting a standard for what others influenced you to be. Many times, material success is often the holy grail of the battle. The comparison to others has to be rooted in things that can be obtained or manipulated. Think about some of the things you've strived for. Grades, cars, homes, job titles, vacations, etc. Many of these can be desires of your own but oftentimes your preferences can be influenced by how you think you'll be perceived with those possessions.

They are all things that signify that you've been a winner in some form. Many of them actually indicated that you've beaten out someone else or performed better in your career or business. Those can be great moments that shape your life in positive ways but remember that the *law of diminishing returns* will probably have the last say in those things continuing to be gratifying for you.

Step 2

Write down the moments in which you were acknowledged or celebrated for outperforming others. Grab a sheet of paper and list them out. Seriously, this page isn't going anywhere. MAKE THE LIST!

After you get stuck and can't think of more. Read each one and try to determine what that moment did for your self esteem or confidence.

Here's a few curveball questions:
1.   Why is public acknowledgement or adulation such an important pillar in your self esteem?
2.   Is it healthy to allow your confidence to be rooted in comparison or recognition?

Step 3

"Goal" is such a loaded word. There's a general belief that we should have goals in order to have direction in our lives. However, there's typically a limited amount of education on how to position yourself with goals.

Goals are blissful intentions. At the core, they are optional. When you set a goal. You naturally are creating space for potentially not achieving it. It's literally in the definition.

Goal - the object of a person's <u>ambition</u> or effort; an aim or desired result.

This definition implies that there's a chance it won't happen. "Aim", "desired", etc. A goal is nice for direction but at this stage of life you need standards. You need to have non-negotiables in place that require you to be your highest self in each moment.

In the aforementioned steps, I said "determine your goals for war" because the goal word is common speak. I'm sure you want the real, you want to elevate your life. Replace the idea of your desires as being "goals", honor them as standards or requirements. Watch how some of your behaviors, actions, and thoughts become unacceptable when you view your aspirations as requirements instead of "nice to have". Don't run from that accountability. The healthiest thing you could do is embrace this concept. Your dreams are not bigger than you. You possess dreams, they don't possess you. Stand on them in full confidence! How would you ever experience something that you don't take a stance of ownership with?

Step 4

Trust. Big trust! That's a scary word. So much disappointment and pain has come after the word *trust*. Trusting others is a slippery slope. It can lead to moments of love and honor while it could also cause despair and grief. There's no instruction manual or crystal ball for knowing exactly who or what to trust.

Here's a great place to start; trust yourself. You may have let yourself down before but you are also the only person you can control. You have a greater sense of how you'll show up for yourself.

Now, what do you have to trust yourself with? Commitment. Another word that brings up angst. *Commitment is staying true to what you said you would do long after the mood that you said it in has left.*

The internal wins are what you have to commit to. Let me give you a few examples of internal wins:
- Saying "no" when you need time or space to rest and recover
- Going to the gym and making yourself uncomfortable in the moment in order to have a healthier future

- Celebrating yourself for honoring a new bed time
- Making time to enjoy your favorite hobbies even when your peers don't enjoy them

These are examples of things that could help you exhibit a new level of self love. The list can be endless but you get the point. You have to "do you" in order to be fulfilled. Those that love YOU will understand. Those that use you will complain. Stay diligent in winning your war!

Chapter 4 - Ditching the Escape Plan

There's no dollar amount that can buy you out of regret. You cannot run from the journey that will calm your soul. There are instances when you may have chosen the promotion over leaving the job to pursue a world-changing idea or gift. The raise could surely meet your financial needs at the moment however are you foregoing mental or emotional peace for more dollars?

It's not abnormal to put yourself in a position to earn more of the resource that affords you necessities, lifestyle, and enjoyment. However, if money is the only form of abundance that you recognize, there is a chance that you only view your life as a process of having enough money to escape your current responsibilities. Growing your definition of abundance can shift your mission from escaping the discomforts of a job that you dislike to inviting new opportunities that bring peace and prosperity to you in ways that you have not fathomed.

Life is not about escaping, it's about allowing. Allowing what? Allowing your heart to receive abundance in forms that your mind is not equipped to recognize.

Prime example, imagine sitting in traffic multiple times per week arguing with yourself about why you have to go to work despite the mental and emotional stress it creates within you. Playing your favorite music during the commute is just a distraction, a coping mechanism to enjoy 30 minutes of hyping yourself up to complete a day full of tasks that aren't fulfilling to you. Every time you catch yourself realizing *this ain't it*, you double down on "I have bills to pay."

This cycle is as *toxic* as they come. Repeating this can put you in a space where your closest loved ones become annoying, your favorite outfit doesn't excite you, and your next vacation is never soon enough or long enough when it happens.

Escaping this place in life is not about just quitting a job. This space requires you to accept a mission. A mission that relates to God-given abilities, talents, and thoughts. The job you hate is actually your top investor. The paycheck is very likely the resource that you must become a master of. It can help fund every venture that may fill your heart.

The challenge is often "*how do I start living for me?*" The answer never comes to you all at once. It reveals itself piece by piece when you begin to walk with faith, step by step.

Purpose isn't always sexy

Purpose can be fantasized as a unique life long mission that feels special from Day 1. Another newsflash, it's not.

This is an abrupt way to introduce the takeaway but here it is, what you've defined as "purpose" is task based. As an act that you perform. Purpose cannot be reduced to merely actions that help you feel valuable to others. Purpose can be presence. Purpose can be restraint. Your purpose can be seen by others, yet never noticed by you.

It's important to detach ego-based thoughts from the journey. You must choose to accept that you have played roles in other's lives that you are not aware of. That's purpose in the most powerful form.

Imagine you wrestling with emotions that come from thoughts of being inadequate. Shit, scratch *imagine*. You don't need imagination for that. You just need your memory. So, reflect on that. We all leaned into scarcity at some point. We underestimate our positive impact on others simply because it's not always stated or brought to our attention. It's not your fault that self belief was not impressed into your habits as a child, however it's your responsibility to fix that. Let me guess, that's "easier said than done". Well, let's move past the current realities that you have learned to be comfortable in.

The concept of escaping circumstances sounds great until you learn that running is a temporary fix. There's no need to run when you are capable of standing in the circumstance and conquering it from the inside out. Let's get into why it's necessary to overcome your desire to run from situations that seem uncomfortable!

Belief is powerful, it's an extension of faith. When you have faith (noun), you're inclined to believe (verb).

Money is Awful Getaway Driver

My career in finance has shown me something I never believed while growing up. Having more money, itself, does not fill emotional gaps. The underlying thought or belief that lives throughout society is that "if I had more money life would be better." Let me insert a slight edit. "If I had more money the quality of things in my life would be better."

Your life is much bigger than things. Yes, you deserve to have the best. That's not up for debate. However, that's a small part of the equation if your new standard for life is to live within a wholeness and completeness that attracts any of the financial resources you need.

Life is a spiritual and emotional experience at its core. The physical experiences are a byproduct of the spiritual and emotional experiences that are placed in your life to spark growth and learning along your journey.

You're in a dangerous space if your belief system aligns with something physical to be the foundation of your emotional and spiritual experiences. Money or better stated, abundance, can definitely be a thought or spiritual tool before it becomes a physical reality. In fact, abundance starts as an internal feeling before it's ever experienced externally in physical form. This *abundance* can be in the form of an idea, a feeling, an unshakeable knowing. Translation for money purposes; you have to know and feel that you're valuable before value (money) flows into your life.

Money, alone, will not take you to emotional and spiritual levels that you desire. You've seen time and time again that some people with large amounts of money experience misery. You must establish a deeply rooted understanding in your value that money cannot measure or match. The question is often "how?" We'll dive into that next but you must bring the willingness to remove money from the driver's seat.

Finding Fulfillment Beyond Financial Circumstances

In the relentless pace of money-driven societies like the US, money is frequently heralded as the universal key to fulfillment. Yet, true mental, emotional, and spiritual freedom often begins with a decision that transcends your financial standing. A commitment to being bigger than one's circumstances, at least in the realm of thought, is a requirement to *pass go and collect $200.*

Here are a few strategies that have proven to help cultivate this internal strength and confidence, allowing you to pursue genuine personal values and goals even amidst financial pressure.

1. Embrace Reflective Therapy

The journey to fulfillment often involves revisiting moments in our past that have shaped our current mindset. Reflective therapy can be an effective tool for uncovering and healing suppressed emotions and thoughts, especially those rooted in childhood experiences. By addressing these hidden influences, you can begin to rewrite their narratives, empowering yourself to pursue what genuinely makes you feel whole.

In therapy, you create a safe space to reflect on your life's trajectory—where you've been, where you are, and where you aim to be. At first, you may not know how to set an expectation for what you would get from therapy. That's fine! Sometimes the discomfort in trying it is actually a signal that it's a growth step. The reflective practice in therapy builds emotional strength and lays the groundwork for aligning your goals with your true self, independent of financial metrics. In today's world, technology has made it possible to get access to no-cost and low cost counseling or therapy sessions. You deserve to have a clear mind as you elevate to the next level. Trust the assistance that's available because you may need help seeing blindspots.

2. Cultivate Inner Strength through Mental Work

Focused thought is a powerful practice to engage with your inner thoughts and beliefs. Set aside time for regular introspection, allowing you to explore what truly matters to you beyond monetary success. Do you have a quiet place to retreat to or a solo activity? It can be that time sitting in the car once you arrive home. It could be in the shower. Or as you lay in bed before or after sleep. You just need a quiet moment to think about what you think about. This practice can lead to profound insights, fostering a sense of purpose and direction.

During these reflective sessions, consider writing down your takeaways or meditating on what brings you joy and fulfillment. Through this deep and conscious reflection, you can identify personal values and goals that resonate with your intrinsic self, building the inner strength required to pursue them despite external financial constraints.

3. Develop Delusional Confidence

Put on your cape. You need to save yourself! To step beyond the limitations of your current circumstances, sometimes you need to develop what might seem like delusional confidence. No one is equipped to save you but you. You know yourself better than any other person. You are equipped with the ability to hold a belief in your self-worth and capabilities that defies your present situation. Even if it's just for a couple of minutes at first. Making a routine of this detachment from reality gives you time to rebuild your identity. By nurturing this bold, almost illogical belief in your potential, you can navigate the path less trodden, leading to common goals of abundance and well-being shared by many.

This degree of confidence calls for envisioning your ideal self and acting in alignment with that vision. Keyword, *act*. It involves taking calculated risks, embracing failure as part of growth, and maintaining resilience in the face of setbacks. Through this process, you build a bridge between your aspirations and reality, a vital step in realizing fulfillment.

4. Release Logical Structures, Seek Spiritual Wholeness

In pursuing what fulfills you, it is sometimes necessary to abandon the confines of logic and rationality. While sound financial planning is crucial, the path to personal fulfillment may require you to follow your intuition and passions, even when they defy conventional wisdom. This is when advice from others falls short. Again, the journey of fulfillment is a journey of trusting yourself enough to follow your heart or a calling.

Seek experiences that nourish your soul—whether through art, music, nature, travel, contribution to others, or spiritual practices. These endeavors contribute to a sense of spiritual wholeness, offering an anchor that grounds you in what truly makes you feel alive. Harnessing that true sense of life will give you a level of energy that is undeniable. Opportunities will begin to find you. The right people will begin to seek you out. By prioritizing these pursuits, you create a life enriched with meaning that will create a path for financial success.

Overall, finding fulfillment in a world preoccupied with financial gain involves looking inward and valuing personal growth as much as, if not more than, monetary achievement. Through therapy, reflective practices, developing delusional confidence, and seeking spiritual wholeness, individuals can cultivate resilience and authenticity. This approach allows for achieving personal values and goals, creating a life of abundance in dimensions that money cannot measure.

Escaping the "purpose journey" does not grant true freedom. An escape is only temporary and it can only grants our ego with a short lived win. A win that often becomes a regret. Consider this, ditch the escape plan. It's a distraction from your mission here in this life experience.

Peace is found in being the truest version of you. Your gifts will always make room for you!

Questions to Explore:

- Do I believe that winning the lottery will fix the most important things in my life?
- If meaningful relationships are strained now, is my expectation that having more money will automatically fix the relationship? *(sidenote: do not overlook the relationship you have with yourself)*
- Am I willing to accept the idea that I may attract financial abundance while pursuing a calling that is not typically associated with money?
- Do I run from situations that I'm strong enough to change while living in them?

Chapter 5 - God in You

Your purpose is rooted in something that may or may not create financial gain for you. The idea that your purpose is connected to your career or livelihood is misleading. Yes, the need for shelter, food, and nourishment are real. However, your role in co-creating experiences and moments that are shared with others will always create material gain. Your purpose could provide emotional, spiritual, or physical enjoyment for others. The way you make money could simply create the stability for you to positively impact people in a variety of ways. Let's make this simple. Creation is your purpose. This is a role you cannot denounce or detach from it. You're locked into it whether you like it or not. The details of what you create lies within your will to decide how to use your talents, gifts, and opportunities.

What cannot be denied is that you're a creator. You were made in the image of God, therefore you carry some of the characteristics of the creator.

You possess life, an essence, that itself proves you were created therefore you have the ability to create too. All forms of offspring have genes or characteristics of those that procreated. In this basic example, you must accept that there's a piece of God in you. God is not outside of you.

This understanding changes how you view yourself and your worthiness for abundance. You're a representative or extension of a power that created the universe we live in.

Fear, doubt, and even your environment can rob you of this reality. It's easy to slip in a way of life that's driven by *lack* when you do not lean on the fact that abundance is your birthright. Yes, you can decide to create or manifest any material success based on your innate connectedness with the creator.

Unfortunately, the people in your life and environments in which you've found yourself can distract from the knowing the God is in you. Not above, beside, near, or far. A piece of God resides in you.

I am the master of money, I am master of myself, I master all things that concern me

One of the essential steps of improving your life in any area is having the knowing that you will rise above challenges. It's imperative that your belief system leans toward the idea that challenges create growth instead of challenges lead to failure. Make no mistake, both can be true. This is where your will to decide plays a role.

There could be a slight discomfort in reading the highlighted quote today. Your conscious mind (or intellect) may tell you, you have not mastered money. However, your spirit knows that all things were created for you to use for your good.

You are an extension of an infinite power. Therefore, you cannot lack anything. You may have been convinced that you lack things but that's a condition of the mind and not the truth of the heart.

Think about this, how has money been pitted as the problem? It's simply a tool. Would you call a hammer a problem? Hey guys, I have a hammer problem. Absolutely. You could say I haven't learned how to use a hammer correctly. Now, replace "hammer" with "money" in that last sentence.

Abundance is your birthright. In our human experience, we lack nothing. All things that we need are available to us, just in ways we may not be aware of.

The common thought is "I need to make more money". This thought comes from a mental place in which you know you are worthy of more. However, there are some words in that quote that create resistance. Specifically, "need" and "make". You have all that you need right now. If you did not, you probably wouldn't have the opportunity to read this right now. Secondly, you do not make money. It's a matter of how much you allow to come to you through the decisions you make. Let's swap some of the words in that sentence…

I will allow more money into my life.

Instantly, your desire is leading the way instead of positioning yourself to be in need. The money already exists, you do not have to make it. You simply have to allow it in your life by being a fuller version of you that accepts abundance.

The shift is yours to claim. There's nothing that can stop you from thinking differently. It's a choice.

Free yourself of pain. It's challenging based on how we've learned to easily accept pain and question happiness. The mental conditioning that the world has performed must be reversed by you!

Why are winners so admired in society? Is it because winning is viewed as something that's reserved for a select few?

You're a winner and not in the participation trophy way. You've endured challenges, strived for greatness, navigated lows, yet you are still facing each day with a level of resilience that's admirable. You are undefeated in life simply because nothing has stopped you.

You may have admired and respected obstacles for too long. The honor must go to you instead. Your power to get up has proven to be much stronger than the things that have caused you to fall.

You do NOT need permission to live a great life. Ask yourself, "Am I going to wait on things to happen for me when I have the power to create results?"

There's true power in the questions you ask yourself. Based on how we were taught, our confidence has been based on having the right answer. This is misleading and can cause confusion. In your formative years, the right answers led to A's and B's which was success in school. However, that's the method of learning what to think/know instead of how to think! In order to reach new levels you must trust the deeper knowing you possess. Your conscious thinking is good but your subconscious thinking is great. You plant new seeds by presenting yourself with better questions and allowing your mind to work on them in the background. This is just one of the powers you have that will help you reach new heights.

Overall, your power is limitless and "now" is always yours. Open your heart to receive and allow your mind to work. The past is simply a former "now" that can provide wisdom and strength but that must be your focus! Failures only exist if that's how you choose to view the learning moments you've experienced!

Your actions will always align with the level of excellence or worthiness you envision for yourself. The concept of self work is the process that includes awareness, acceptance, and elevation.

You must first become aware of where you are in your personal journey of growth. After becoming aware of your position in life, there is power in accepting it. Acceptance is not defeat. You are accepting that there is more work to do. Work that will improve how you value your own decisions, how you value your future self, and you value your ability to grow.

Only after awareness and acceptance can you elevate yourself. The opposition to these two elements is ignorance and denial. You must choose to separate yourself from these two things. It is an ongoing challenge. There is comfort in ignorance. It's even recognized as bliss. Denial is easy. You take the position of blaming other things and people for your outcomes.

Elevation is not a common result for those that embody these low level states of mind.

   Challenge yourself to be grateful for who you are today and to accept the journey ahead. Choose to view yourself as those that admire who you are and who you're becoming.

Chapter 6 - Using Your Time

Time is life. Yes, time is much more than money. Money is replaceable. There's definitely a connection between time and money but it's overstated. Reducing time to being something that goes hand in hand with money is a slippery slope. This can influence you to have beliefs that cause you to avoid investing time simply because you don't see the immediate monetary return.

Your impact on the lives of others is up to you. You can look at your dreams as "one day..." or you can look at your dreams like it's "Day one". You decide.

You live in a world where time is a precious commodity. You are constantly bombarded with endless distractions, responsibilities, and obligations. Social media, work, bills, etc. can become overwhelming. In the midst of a seemingly chaotic and fast-paced lifestyle, it can be easy to lose sight of your goals or aspirations. You may often find yourself wondering where all the time has gone and why you haven't achieved the things you set out to do. But what if I told you that by rethinking your approach to time and setting priorities, you can eliminate unnecessary tasks and focus on what truly adds value to your life? Think about it like this, you <u>use</u> time. You no longer can look at it as something you spend.

Right now, you would unconsciously say you *spend* your time working, traveling, or leading your family. Look to make time something you use as an **investment** into the positive ideas you carry in your heart and mind. You're in the driver's seat and you have a license to prosper.

Each day, you get 86,400 seconds to grow, love, build, and prosper. Depending on your surroundings, you could be met with negativity, doubt, or fear.

Another Newsflash: You don't have to engage with the negative energy when you have boundaries.

You can acknowledge negativity but you can choose to not tussle with it. You don't have to respond to the hateful comment on social media. You are not required to respond to a toxic text. You can elect to remove yourself from a manipulative conversation. Again, you choose how you use your time and those things typically come with a poor return on your investment of time (and energy).

Your time is better used exploring effective ways to be purposeful and productive with your time in order to achieve meaningful, impactful goals.

This is just a glimpse at why it's important to rethink the way you view time. Time is not something to be managed or controlled. It's a finite resource that cannot be replenished. Instead of trying to cram as many tasks as possible into a day, it's crucial to prioritize and be intentional with your time. This mindset shift is the first step towards effective time management.

Setting priorities is crucial in utilizing time effectively. Ask yourself: what are the top three things that I want to achieve in my life? These can be personal, career, financial or relationship goals.

Your level of focus on the positive aspects within your life can determine the quality of each day. You need as many positive moments as possible to help us overcome the challenges that lead to personal growth. There are moments when you may forget that your experiences are either adding or subtracting from your happiness.

Rethinking your priorities and eliminating unnecessary tasks are essential steps in using our time effectively. Again, in today's fast-paced world, time is truly a valuable commodity and it is imperative that you make the most of it.

It's a challenge to find the words to truly explain time. In a few moments, you will need to explore effective ways to be more purposeful and productive in order to achieve meaningful goals in life.

Firstly, it's crucial to rethink your priorities and your investment of time. Often, you'll get caught up in the daily grind and lose sight of what truly matters to you. Take a step back and assess your current priorities. Are they aligned with your long-term goals and values? If not, it's time to make some changes. This could mean delegating tasks that are not vital or saying "no" to activities that do not contribute to your overall goals. By rethinking your priorities, you can focus our time and energy on what holds true significance in our lives.

Don't let the things that weren't meant to distract you, keep you from growing each day!

Another important realization, you do not have to fight the past to win in the future.

Here's how you've been fighting the past...

- Harping on past decisions
- Thinking about how things would be different if you could go back in time
- Punishing yourself for the path you've traveled

All of those thoughts do not serve who you are becoming. Simply put, it's wasted energy. How? In those scenarios, you're focusing on who you WERE. What about who you ARE or who you WILL BE? You must prioritize those two versions of you.

Your level of belief in who you are becoming determines everything. The only limit to who you will be is the one you set. If anything, question why you decide to not believe in greater outcomes in the future. After all, it's a decision. It could be an unconscious one, yet it's a decision.

The mental shift that will serve you most is believing that you are bigger than any challenge. The best path to embracing this belief is to disconnect from past experiences. You aren't there anymore. As Tony Robbins says, "The past does not equal your future… unless you live there."

Next, it is important to eliminate any distractions or tasks that do not add value to your life or those in your life. This could include mindless scrolling through social media, attending meetings that do not require your presence, or engaging in toxic relationships/conversations. These distractions not only take up your time but also drain you mentally and emotionally. By eliminating them, we free up space and time.

Your thoughts could easily slip into the "easier said than done" space at the idea of eliminating the various distractions in life. That's exactly where you may need to start!

Questions to explore:
- Why am I so quick to think that self improvement is hard?
- Would it serve me to think that the decision to stay the same is simple as the decision to evolve?

What are common things you invest your time into?	How does the activity impact you or others?
Examples: TV shows, gardening, recreational sports, parenting, working out, etc...	*Examples: It allows me step away of life's responsibilities for a moment, Helps me build a connection with others*

Tip: Do not include your main occupation or job

Time can be attached to money but time is <u>not</u> money! How you use time says a lot about your belief system. Writing down where your time goes is a practice to build awareness!

Chapter 7 - Trusting Alignment

You Are Going to Save You

You are the leader that you've been looking for. You will reroute your course in order to better enjoy the journey. It's you that holds the power. Unfortunately, others may fall short of your newly set standard of excellence. That's ok because there's usually a small group of individuals that change the world for everyone else. You must accept that you're a part of that group when you choose self improvement.

The choice to become better, stronger, or wiser gives you the title of "leader". Leadership starts with where you direct yourself, not others. You can no longer look at the lack of leadership in others as a disappointment. That indicates that you are not focusing on the things you can control. Do not lose sight of the idea that your choices and behaviors may be the catalyst to others' healthier choices. You will attract those that can support you in your journey by first committing to lead yourself.

Are you willing to embrace the idea of being first to a party? You choose the music, you choose the decor, you choose the dress code, you ensure that you enjoy the moment. The first few minutes may feel lonely and awkward but the night will prove to be most memorable. Lead with no doubt!

The shift to be more understanding and patient with yourself is worth it. It's not easy to break the habit of being critical of yourself. You must acknowledge that

it may be a habit that was passed to you from others that were critical of you.
- "I should have…"
- "Why didn't I…"
- "I'm always missing out on.."

The list could continue for all of the ways that you might criticize yourself, knowingly or unknowingly. There's a thin line between self accountability and critique. You can accept the responsibility of making improvements as you move forward without shunning yourself based on past decisions.

Take a moment to ask yourself "what do you gain from criticizing yourself?" Once you identify that there aren't many, if any, benefits then there's an opportunity to see the habit for what it is, a distraction. Anything that gets in the way of you loving yourself is a distraction.

How could you still doubt yourself when you've successfully overcome every obstacle in your entire life?

This question brings a perspective to your life that minimizes doubt! Throughout life challenges will arise. Accept it. Growth is planted in challenges. Be willing to investigate the doubts and worries that fill your mind. Your mind will dabble in areas that seem logical but are not. It is logical to think more about the worst case scenario than the best case scenario? Maybe. Does this habit serve who you could become? No.

Using caution is a more powerful approach than exercising fear (from doubt/worry) however fear seems to dominate, why? The baseline is typically "what do I need to do to avoid pain or discomfort?" That's understandable. That approach is what we call survival mode.

Survival mode is not known to be enjoyable. The dreams and ambitions, most importantly a sense of freedom, are often experienced by those that are in position to thrive. The lifelong quest is to live life in a way that begets ease.

The first and most difficult step is to recalibrate the thoughts that you associate with the triumphs and successes you want to see in it. Your thoughts of "what you want" and "why you want them" are most helpful. The thoughts of "how" seem logical but overly indulging in these can actually stifle progress. Simply due the fact that you may not have an immediate answer to "How" you'll achieve or create something. Without that answer, a feeling of doubt or worry forms. This feeling does not lead to confident actions that precede the desired result.

You must not forget that you are undefeated in life when it comes to obstacles. You've successfully overcome them despite the odds. Let's not voluntarily choose to doubt things mentally when your spirit knows nothing but win.

> *Not being happy with "life" is actually you not being happy with a particular situation in life*

Perspective is what determines your life experience. Thankfully, you have the largest influence on your outlook.

It's common to think that you are not happy with your life however this is not the case. Life itself is a blessing no matter what your conditions or circumstances are. Where you may be experiencing challenges or hurdles is with a situation in life.

This simple shift in perspective can change how you approach everything! A discussion about "surrender" led to this quote being the Monday motivation. We collectively summarized surrender as the acceptance of what is, which provides the foundation to take positive action to improve the quality of things, relationships, or activities in your life.

The mind can create stories that exaggerate negatives and dismiss positives simply because you've been taught to value imperfection. Think about it. What have you done (or do) to fix or avoid what you perceive as an "imperfection" in your life? The mere fact that many of your actions are rooted in fixing or avoiding things means you prioritize the imperfection to a point that you try to correct it to become more valuable.

What if it wasn't an imperfection, what if you could experience happiness despite it? These imperfections or perceived shortcomings are just situations IN life. They are not YOUR life. No matter what happens or what may be true at this very moment, your life is precious, valuable, unique, and inspiring.

Live with the energy of triumph. You've already won the life lottery by just existing.

> *If you want to prosper, you must love prosperity in all forms*

How many times have you criticized abundance that wasn't yours? Have you ever diminished someone's prosperity because you believed that they didn't deserve it? Has anyone ever taught you that having more than enough was ungodly?

Prosperity must be something you admire, encourage, and appreciate if you want to be aligned with it yourself. How could you condemn something that you want to attract? That's not how the laws of life work.

I challenge you to compliment people that are experiencing abundance in the ways that you want it for yourself. Bless them for living on a level that you're on your way to.

The expectation that life, itself, will change your experience is a baseless expectation. You often get what you're looking for whether it's problems or solutions. Throughout life you may have been exposed to unhealthy examples that you ultimately added or modeled in your own life. Again, this is not your fault but you have a responsibility to find better ways to operate.

What's an example of this? Verbally saying you want better opportunities and solutions but energetically focusing on the problems. In your experience, you may have only learned to focus on problems because that's what fixes them. Actually, focusing on solutions eliminates problems.

Ironically, you may feel justified in highlighting the problems. Acknowledging the reasons why something is not working may seem like the logical thing to do. It puts the onus on the circumstance rather than you. This allows you to meet life in a way that feels free of guilt or responsibility.

"I haven't started saving because the bills keep coming every month". This statement has truth but it also gives more power to the bills than your ability to grow in ways that minimize the impact of bills. This is an example of meeting life in a way where you believe things/circumstances are larger than you.

You must meet life in a different way. As someone that can grow, adapt, and overcome regardless of the obstacle. If there is a feeling that declaring ease and abundance over your life seems delusional you have to question where your beliefs are. The practice of expecting greatness from yourself should be the norm. The obstacles just contribute to your story of triumph. They are not to be respected as things that have more power than you.

Life meets you as you meet it. Think twice about what you believe has power over how you experience life.

Trust, it won't feel *fair.* When you have to accept the things you can't control and operate at a high level despite those hurdles, you will feel like you have to give what you haven't received... yet.

In creating this habit/practice, you'll begin to notice that in these situations in the past you've been negative for no reason. You might have created fictitious stories in your mind on how the means to someone's abundance was not honest or noble. This is called a spirit of lack. When you see levels of prosperity and abundance that you desire, there must be a positive mood that comes over you. You've witnessed more evidence that your reality can be the same. However, if you first look to create reasons why someone else shouldn't have something you desire, you have actually uncovered a reality that you might be uncomfortable with accepting. You have shown that you have a lack of belief in obtaining things therefore it's hard for you to believe someone has possessed certain things rightfully.

There must be a love for prosperity no matter who the beneficiary is. It's your nature that you must correct in order for your reality to shift. Use this week to compliment abundance using the voice in your mind. This will begin to welcome it into your own life!

Relationships

Are you placing value on creating new relationships? Imagine every person you encounter has a gift for you. However, the only way to receive the gift is to consider that this person's role is to change or improve your life. It could be in a small way or big way, you do not decide that.

People are the representatives of opportunity. Think about it. Suggestions, referrals, introductions, etc are all made by people in your life. Every new journey or path you could embark on requires people at some point.

We also have learned that the decisions of others can be a source of our pain or uncertainty. As a popular saying goes, "people will either be a lesson or a blessing". Life requires us to navigate that possibility at all times.

Here's the beauty in it… You set the boundaries to how people can impact your life with the energy that you carry. You can operate with a sense of "elevated determination" that no one can reach or shake. Alternatively, you can choose to have "impressionable confidence" that someone's negativity can feast on.

The right people align with elevated determination. Why? Simply because those that have convinced themselves of their own dreams are the same people that can inspire you to stay committed to yours. No one you meet is by accident. People will help you confirm if you've set your boundaries correctly.

What's Alignment?

Alignment with your highest self is not a mere milestone to be achieved, it is an ongoing journey, a steadfast commitment to the process of becoming your truest self. It is often full of challenges. Life might appear to be an uphill battle, particularly through the lens of others who perceive your aspirations as unrealistic. In reshaping these external narratives, you may feel the world nudging you toward complacency, urging you to temper your dreams with so-called realism. It's a trap! It is imperative that you resist this wave of realism. Trust that the true essence of enlightenment lies in answering the call of your innermost desires.

In this journey, self-talk becomes a vital tool. The words you whisper to yourself can either be the chains that bind you or the wings that set you free. The voice inside you, the one that dares to dream beyond limits, must be your most trusted companion. It knows the vision you hold in your heart and the impact you yearn to make. Affirm its message, especially when others dismiss your ambitions as "crazy".

Every day offers an opportunity to align with this vision, and it is through this alignment that transformative experiences unfold. The responsibility is constant, as is the reward. A richer, more authentic life awaits you. Imagine standing at the twilight of your life, burdened not with regret but elevated by a legacy of bold adventures and the serene knowledge that you pursued your truth.

Embrace this inner journey as a creative endeavor. Allow the process to inspire, to drive you beyond the confines of conventional wisdom. Trust that each step, no matter how uncertain, is part of a grander tapestry of self-discovery. Let go of the notion that your path must mirror those before you. Instead, pioneer your own, fueled by the unique visions crafted in the quiet recesses of your mind, body, and soul.

In trusting the process of alignment, you unlock the potential to rewrite your narrative, to live in a space where possibility knows no bounds. It's here, within this trust, that enlightenment grows. Write your story with bold strokes, for it is yours alone to tell.

Chapter 8 - Protect The Mission

Your job is simple. Protect your mission and embrace your journey.

We are ALWAYS in the process of creating a new life. However, the events in life may cause us to be less aware of this fact at times. We must acknowledge that each result or outcome, positive or negative, is a product of a thought we chose. (Yes, read that again). The formula looks something like this.

Thoughts -> Feelings -> Actions -> Results

That's a powerful formula but it also represents a supreme level of accountability. Each day is an opportunity to improve how we use the formula to grow. We must choose to clean up our thoughts in order to see the results in our lives change. Simply said, the conditioning we've received throughout life must be challenged. The cliche sayings, the small mindedness, the self sabotage must stop! We must unlearn the programming that has been embedded in us since adolescence. Many of the thoughts we experience aren't even our own. They were passed to us from others. You know what that means, we're carrying the trauma of friends, relatives, and associates that have planted thoughts in us that don't serve our desires.

Luckily, you've chosen to live as your higher self. The fact that you are reading this means you moved on a thought of prosperity and growth. You decided that financial limitations were no longer going to be the "result" you settle for. The decision to become a wealth builder must be rooted in the idea that you're already wealthy and that the reality around you is simply catching up. Your only job is to maintain the habit of allowing the better thoughts to lead you despite what your current circumstances may be!

What thoughts would you focus on when you wake up knowing abundance flows endlessly to you?

You cannot wait for evidence before you believe in being and having more. The evidence appears only when you first accept an idea as being real. Wealth is not a number in your bank account. It is a state of being. Not doing, BEING. The moment you step into this state the world will bend to reflect it back to you.

You probably assume that being clear and confident is a favorable state, right? Does a confident person maintain habits of worry or doubt? No, they expect great things and often receive them. There is an unshakable confidence that precedes true growth.

If you wish to create abundance or a sense of freedom, you have to feel it first. You cannot create something that you have not already possessed. Here's the breakdown...

Creation is actually a form of duplication. You're recreating (or duplicating) a thought just into a physical reality. Feeling abundant and confident is a *right now* project. It's not reserved for tomorrow or when your circumstances change. If you believe that you can't *feel* abundance until it's physically present, you may be living within a cycle of a limiting belief. It's your job to assume the feeling of which everything you desire is already present in your life. This is not as challenging as it seems. Your thoughts are a part of your life too. Therefore, if you can fathom abundance you already have it in one form.

The bigger question is where did you learn that your thoughts were separate from your reality? Who declared that only tangible things can be categorized as "real".

Stop telling the story of struggle. Stop claiming lack. That behavior is beneath your highest self. You must act in accordance with your highest self if you want to experience the physical reality of your highest desires. All of the words that you speak are full of certainty. You may not think so because you're aware of the context of saying something jokingly or as a habit. However, your subconscious mind does not operate with context. It receives all thoughts and words as literal or true.

When you see a big price tag, do not choose to shrink to the level of your obstacles. You must choose to affirm that you can afford anything you desire. No one is going to make that correction for you. That's your work to complete. Even if your circumstances do not seem like they're changing, your inner shift will ultimately demand that the external world reflect that shift. The people, opportunities, and events that are required to match your inner reality will present themselves without much effort.

Inventory check! In this case, your mental inventory. Look for the reasons behind the thoughts you have or continuously recycle. This process will unpack two things. Either fear or love.

Over time, the conditions around you reflect the conditions of your mind. For example, your stress levels can increase simply from a thought. The potential of an unwanted outcome can put you in a state of "fight or flight" mode before it even takes place.

The question that must be answered is why would I think thoroughly about an unwanted outcome. The justification is typically some form of *"I want to be prepared if things go wrong"*. That's an understandable approach if you're relying on fear to best prepare you for life. This can provide solace in terms of survival but the various results from this line of thinking will rarely bring bliss. "A fear state cannot produce enjoyment" in the words of Tony Robbins.

The question that empowers your inventory check is *"What if I prepare myself for things to go right?"*. Granted, your survival instincts may not want to let go of the wheel. You must decide to let abundance thinking have a say. What would change about where you live, who you look to connect with, what you use money for, etc. if your mental set point was on positive possibilities instead of mere survival?

Love for ascension has to be more powerful in your mind than the fear of falling. In every instance where you've accepted a failure as the end of your success story, it later becomes apparent that there was a seed being planted for a pivot. Sometimes, the pivot is your attitude instead of the goal. Ever fail a test? Instead of never taking it again, you studied differently and more intentionally. Same goal, but failure enhanced the approach.

Fear of failure is overrated. Love the process and its hurdles. It's the mental state that manufactures all great things. Therefore, look at yourself as an unstoppable being. No need to fear what makes you stronger. Focus on the love for who you've become in your journey. The world and surroundings have no choice but to reflect what's inside of you. Manage your inventory!

There comes a moment when you have to stop doubting what you already know deep down. You've felt it stirring in you—that quiet inner nudge that keeps showing up, even when you try to push it aside. Maybe you've labeled it as unrealistic. Maybe you've told yourself it's just a phase, or that you'll get to it "when things settle down." But it keeps coming back, doesn't it?

That's not a coincidence. That's purpose.

And here's the truth: you don't need anyone else to confirm it for you. You don't need another sign, another degree, or another plan. What you need is to believe in what's already inside you. That desire you keep suppressing? That dream you're afraid to say out loud? That's real. It matters. And it's time to stop treating it like a side thought.

I get it—you're tired. You've been carrying a lot, balancing a lot, trying to be everything to everyone. Maybe you've gotten good at pushing your own needs to the side while you handle the immediate, the practical, the urgent. But you can't keep ignoring your calling without it eventually catching up to you. It's not going to let you go.

You were made for more—not because what you've done so far isn't enough, but because there's something greater waiting on the other side of your yes. And no, it won't be perfect. It won't be easy. But it will be worth it. You don't have to have every answer before you begin. You just need to trust that your next step is enough for now.

Start with what you have. Use what you know. Give yourself permission to begin, even if the beginning feels messy or unclear. That's how purpose works; it unfolds as you move, not before. The clarity you're craving? It comes in motion, not in waiting.

You're not behind. You haven't missed your moment. What's meant for you didn't pass you by—it's been waiting for you to be ready to receive it. And readiness isn't about having it all figured out. It's about being willing to listen to that voice inside you and take one courageous step at a time.

You're allowed to want more. You're allowed to change direction. You're allowed to grow beyond the version of yourself other people got used to. This is your life. You don't owe anyone an explanation for choosing alignment, healing, or joy.

And if you're scared? That's okay. Courage doesn't mean the absence of fear—it means choosing to move anyway. Purpose isn't a feeling you chase; it's a decision you commit to. And right now, you get to decide.

So take the leap. Say yes to yourself. Say yes to the dream you keep trying to quiet. Yes to the story that keeps rising up inside you. Yes to the life that fits who you really are—not just who you've had to be.

You're capable. You're ready. You're not alone.

This is your time.

Go make the shift. Go build the thing. Go speak the truth. Go live the kind of life that lets your soul breathe.

You don't need more permission. You've been locked into your purpose from Day 1. You're enough and will always be enough.

About the Author

When it comes to creating solutions for life, there aren't many people that compare. Rob Boyd manages to bring together points and examples that help thousands of people navigate personal life, finances, and careers.

In *Prisoner of Purpose*, Rob Boyd puts his creative yet logical approach to common challenges that many experience. Ultimately, equipping you with new perspectives to ambitiously move through the ebbs and flows that life presents. Using real-world examples, Rob sheds light on how anyone can bring value to those in your lives through persistence, belief, and constant improvement.

Rob learned the value of leadership at an early age growing up in North Durham, NC, as the oldest child and team captain in several sports. Rob's dedication, hard work, and determination to avoid a life of poverty and mediocrity inspired him to be more than he saw around him. His path led him to start businesses, lead organizations, and transform people and industries alike.

The insights and wisdom shared in this book were first shared in keynote speaking opportunities at Fortune 500 companies, international economic development forums, universities, and more. Rob Boyd knows that excellence is a journey, not simply a destination, and this book was written to guide you in your commitment to self improvement.

"It's an honor to be locked in on making irreplaceable contributions to the world. Being a prisoner of purpose is a role that creates great things for yourself and others."
Rob Boyd

www.ingramcontent.com/pod-product-compliance
Lightning Source LLC
LaVergne TN
LVHW091316080426
835510LV00007B/515